Donald Yates was born in Jersey City, NJ and graduated from the Choate School in Wallingford, CT in 1958. He then attended the University of Notre Dame in South Bend, IN where he graduated in 1962 with a B.A. degree in English. A short time later, Don joined the United States Peace Corps as an "early" volunteer and served in the Philippine Islands from 1962–1964 as an educator and administrator in a rural community. Upon returning to the United States, he met and married his beautiful wife, "Penny" (Mary Elizabeth Kelly), while beginning his career as an educator teaching English and reading at various private and public schools in northern NJ. He began his administrative work in the Irvington, NJ public schools where he was a Coordinator and a Curriculum Supervisor for nine years. During this time, Don earned his Master's degree in English from Seton Hall University, a Master's degree in Secondary Reading Education from Jersey City State College (now New Jersey City University), and both a third Master's degree and a doctorate in Educational Administration both from Columbia University.

In 1985 Don became a Vice Principal at Millburn High School and then in 1989 became Principal of Leonia High School where he served for nine years before retiring from public education to pursue further administrative work in New Jersey higher education positions as first an Assistant Professor, then an Associate Professor, at Jersey City State College, Caldwell College (now University), and Georgian Court College (now

University). He completed his education career as an Adjunct Professor at Brookdale Community College in 2018 after 56 years in education.

Throughout his long and distinguished career, Don presented materials at many national conferences and conventions, many of these based upon his life-long personal interests of innovative, child-centered educational programs and "Best Practice" concepts involving advanced teacher development and training. He also published a book, *Good Business Sense for Doing Good Business,* a number of articles, and other literature concerning teacher certification, clinical practices, and accelerated teacher preparation programs.

He and his wife, Penny, reside in Shrewsbury, NJ in close proximity to their son and daughter and their four grandchildren.

To my dear friend, classmate, and Peace Corps roommate, Jack Green, whose steadying influence and common-sense decision making kept me focused and involved in my volunteer work.

To my younger brother, Glen Yates, who gave me excellent suggestions on the set up and presentation of the episodes in this book.

Donald Yates

A Journey for Peace: A Journal of Peace

Episodes of Life from an Early Peace Corps Volunteer

Austin Macauley Publishers™
London • Cambridge • New York • Sharjah

All of the events in this memoir are true to the best of author's memory. The views expressed in this memoir are solely those of the author.

Ordering Information
Quantity sales: Special discounts are available on quantity purchases by corporations, associations, and others. For details, contact the publisher at the address below.

Publisher's Cataloging-in-Publication data
Yates, Donald
A Journey for Peace: A Journal of Peace

ISBN 9781638299233 (Paperback)
ISBN 9781638299240 (ePub e-book)

Library of Congress Control Number: 2022922904

www.austinmacauley.com/us

First Published 2023
Austin Macauley Publishers LLC
40 Wall Street, 33rd Floor, Suite 3302
New York, NY 10005
USA

mail-usa@austinmacauley.com
+1 (646) 5125767

To my dear wife and confidant, Penny Yates, who endured many hours of proofreading and textual emendations to clarify the overall direction and presentation of the episodes.

Table of Contents

Preface **11**

Prologue: Culture Shock **15**

Philippine Episodes **21**

"Tex" and His Wife 23

The A.I.D. That Was Lacking Aid 27

Rats Again! 30

Good Old American Ingenuity! 33

The "Monkey Man" and the *Quan* 35

A Play on Language 38

No Shoes/No Service! 41

Shoe Polish – Or Is It? 44

A Boy with Knowledge beyond His Years 47

An Island Trip with "Bottling" Torres 50

A Baptism Surprise with a Fiery Ending 54

The Ears and the Sore Ankles 58

A Very Vivid Funeral 61

Fly FAST, Die Fast 65

Medical Check-Ups 68

"Four Points! Good Grief!" 71

Spectacular Baguio City and Environs 74

In a Pig's Eye to Denvir 80

Bar Fight – Or Not 84

My Ad Hoc Conference Presentation 87

Bilaan Pilot School Graduation: The Highs and The Lows 91

Life With Bindo Alpa 95

Problems and Fatalities 99

"Thoughts" 102

Reflections 104

Epilogue – "Journals of Peace" Presentation 108

Peace Corps Memorabilia 112

Letter from President J. F. Kennedy 113

Invitation from Sargent Shriver 114

Note from Congressman Peter Rodino 115

Letter from Vice President Hubert Humphrey 116

Article from *The Glen Ridge Paper* about Don in the Peace Corps 118

Peace Corps Diploma 122

Preface

In 1961, then-president, John F. Kennedy, set into motion a program of world peace which would affect how we, as Americans, viewed our roles as people who could make a difference. As he so eloquently stated, "Ask not what your country can do for you; ask what you can do for your country." I, and many other young adults, many of college age, took up the challenge and joined the United States Peace Corps. In 1962, as a senior at the University of Notre Dame, I responded to the message presented by a Peace Corps recruiter and signed up to start service just after graduation. I had thoughts of graduate school and either teaching or journalism as an English major, but I was not convinced to move on to these fields just yet. I was assigned to the Philippine Islands, along with a good friend and classmate of mine, and started training within six weeks of school completion.

Our enlistees, assigned to Group VII, met for a three-week training period at San Jose State College (now University), and at the end of that time, our group learned that we would all be assigned to the southern Philippines, and a select few of us were to be assigned to the area below the southern Philippines in the Sulu Sea on the islands of Jolo and Tawi-Tawi. My classmate, Jack, and I were told we would be assigned to the island of Jolo near the town of Jolo City in the small *barrio* of Bilaan. We were contracted to teach English, physical education, and community development.

We completed more training oversees in Manila and still more training in the southern Philippine city of Zamboanga on the big island of Mindanao. The training and indoctrination we had was lacking in many ways as our area of the country was almost entirely Muslim, not Catholic as is the majority of the country's 7,000 islands. We had no languages classes and no cultural training, so we were heading into "uncharted waters." Luckily, the islanders all speak a type of patois English as a way to unify the islands.

I accepted the challenge without hesitation, however, but I began to develop a selfish motive for my commitment. I felt that if I could work for two years in the jungles of the Philippines in leaky-roofed termite-ridden schoolhouses with an extremely wide range of student ages and abilities and then return to the states with a zeal for promoting education, then I would be convinced that teaching is in my blood. It was, and I was an educator in private, public, higher education, and New Jersey State Department roles for over 65 years.

While I worked in the Philippines, I kept a diary of nearly 500 pages, trying to make note of all the daily trials and tribulations that I experienced. As I reviewed my writings, I thought it best to compile situational incidents, or episodes, and work them into a series of vignettes presented herein, as to include my entire diary would display some of the monotony and boredom that oftentimes came upon me as I wrote. These episodes, I feel, will serve as a fitting testimony to my service and to the significance of the sixtieth anniversary of the founding of the Peace Corps.

Don Yates

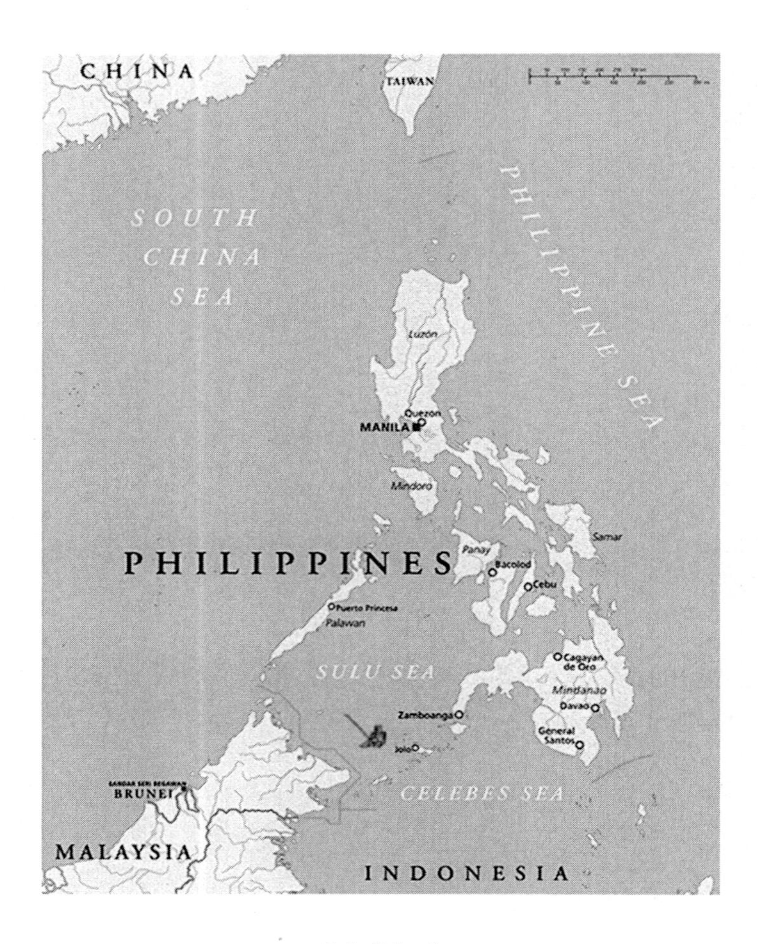
CHINA
TAIWAN
SOUTH
CHINA
SEA
PHILIPPINE SEA
Luzon
Quezon
MANILA
Mindoro
PHILIPPINES
Panay
Bacolod
Samar
Cebu
Puerto Princesa
Palawan
SULU SEA
Cagayan
de Oro
Mindanao
Davao
Zamboanga
General
Santos
Jolo
BRUNEI
CELEBES SEA
MALAYSIA
INDONESIA

Jolo Island

Prologue:
Culture Shock

Hi, my name is Don Yates, and I served as one of the earliest Peace Corps Volunteers from 1962–1964 in the southern Philippine Islands on the island of Jolo where they had not seen a person from the Western Hemisphere, other than missionaries, since their liberation from the Japanese by American forces in 1946. My housemate, Jack, who was a classmate of mine at the University of Notre Dame and persuaded me to accompany him to a session on campus with a Peace Corps recruiter, was an integral part of the following episode, and I thank him often for indirectly saving my life.

My story seems funny now in retrospect, but at the time, it was shocking, almost deadly. The southern area of The Philippines is almost 95% Indonesian Muslim, even though the majority of the country is 95% Catholic. Our little island in the South Seas is actually closer to the mainland of Indonesia, with the largest Muslim population in the world, than it is to the Philippines' larger islands to the north. Many of the customs and religious observances we experienced were new to us, and no one who trained us for our two-year mission knew of the uniqueness of our situation. We had no electricity or running water for our two years, and we were trained to be teachers and community developers, but we had little or no knowledge of the language or the uniqueness of this part of the world. We had been in the country for only four months and were just beginning to get acclimated to our surroundings and our jobs.

On one particular night, near the conclusion of the Month of Ramadan, one of the holiest months in the Muslim calendar, Jack and I had just received an invitation to the house of Mayor Lincoln Tulawie as his seventh wife had just given birth to a baby girl and asked us to come by and see her and have light refreshments. He would have invited us for a full dinner, but during Ramadan, a Muslim must fast from sunrise to sunset and then eat only sparingly otherwise. We were thrilled at this invitation as another one of his wives was the Principal of Bilaan Elementary School where we worked. His house was about two miles down the only road in our barrio of Bilaan, and between our house and his was a military compound manned by the Philippine Constabulary (PC), the local law enforcement group in the area. Interestingly, all PC personnel were Catholic, from northern islands, as it was appropriate then to have non-Muslims in control of the Muslim populace, saving much "bad blood."

Regarding the month of Ramadan, because of fasting and deep devotional periods of each day, many people of the local sect of Islamic faith were extremely frazzled and high-strung at that time. Some of the more zealous devotees actually hallucinated, with the assistance of local drugs, and acted strangely. We later learned that, during Ramadan, if any male member of this sect had a dream in which he saw a white horse riding in the sky, it was a sign to him that the Islamic god, Allah, was summoning him to heaven, and the only way he could achieve "nirvana" was to kill as many non-believers as he could before he, in turn, was killed: it was a kind of ritualized suicide. This action was called "running amok" which is a term we still use today for someone's activities which are odd, weird, and dangerous. Making matters more unusual for the "dreamer", is that he could run amok only on the evening of a full moon and use only a machete as his murder weapon. Furthermore, if a particular male had that dream, all other male members of that person's family had to run amok alongside the "dreamer."

Jack and I began to prepare for our trek to Mayor Tulawie's house, but we were running late as Jack, who had lost over twenty pounds because he could not get used to the exotic food we had to eat, could not find a pair of pants that would fit him. We had heard from our neighbors about the amok tradition, but we had not experienced any incident within the month, so we were preparing to visit the mayor that particular evening without a second thought, as we were so pleased at being invited. Finally, I gave Jack a pair of my pants, and we were set to leave the house. We walked down the few steps from our entranceway to the road and began walking when we heard a series of rifle shots and heard bullets slicing through the banana leaves over our heads. Jack and I dove into the roadside ditch and lay there without moving or talking for many long minutes. Finally, Jack mentioned to me that we could probably go on our way safely, but I said that idea was foolish at this point, and we should get right back home. As we got back inside, more shots rang out, and we then grabbed our two single mattresses, as we were told to do during an amok, and propped them up against our front door for protection while we crouched down behind them and waited.

The next day, many people were out and about, and we slowly began to hear the story of what had transpired. It seems that one Islamic male of this sect had experienced the "dream", and he and two other male members of his family, one being a twelve-year boy, had run amok. They decided to infiltrate the PC campgrounds, as, of course, that's where the so-called non-believers were headquartered. That night, after moonrise, each of them broke through the chicken wire surrounding the camp and advanced toward the barracks. The commanding officer, who knew of the Ramadan tradition well, slept with a pistol under his pillow, but his window was left open, and the eldest male jumped through it. At the last second, the officer grabbed his pistol and shot his attacker. The next oldest male was also shot near another barrack, but the young boy lost his nerve and ran from the PC camp down the road toward our house. It was he whom the PC were shooting at in pursuit as he ran past us. To a member of this sect, coming out of an amok attack alive is almost worse than death as he is shunned by his family and his community, totally ostracized.

Here's where Jack saved my life; if he had found a pair of pants that fit him, he and I, on our trip to the mayor's, would have been right in front of the PC camp when the shooting started! Timing is everything in life…

Days later, after apologies to the mayor who totally understood our situation, we were invited again to his house, this time after the conclusion of Ramadan, for a local feast, which we found out was to be a banquet in our honor. Even though the mayor was not wealthy, he spared no expense and had gone all out to prepare this feast for the Americans. We sat along a large rectangular table and were, at first, served a bowl of hot broth soup, and because there were no utensils, we lifted the bowl to our lips and drank the liquid. After the soup bowls were cleared away, I remarked to the mayor, in my broken dialect, how the clear both was so tasty and how succulent the olive in the soup was. He looked at me in a funny way and said, 'That was no olive. That was the eyeball of a sheep!' I probably then turned many shades of green and wondered what our next course would be. We were then served a fruit salad which was laid out on a large banana leaf for each diner. Since there were no utensils, we knew, from earlier experiences, to use the thumb and two forefingers of our left hand to eat – the left hand only, as the right hand was known as the "impure hand", since it was used for wiping in the outhouse. I must have been the first person finished with this course and, thinking that the banana leaf was a part of the "salad", I proceeded to pick up the leaf and started chewing on it. As each of the others at the table finished the salad, they, too, picked up their banana leaf and started to chew on it. It wasn't until after the meal was over that one of the braver of the guests told me that I had eaten the "plate." Yet, in a gracious fashion typical of Asian countries, each guest began to devour the leaf so that I, the outsider, would "save face!"

Philippine Constabulary Camp in Bilaan

Don with Mayor Lincoln Tulawie

Philippine Episodes

"Tex" and His Wife

After arriving on the island of Jolo for the start of my two-year Peace Corps volunteer work, I was told that the house I was to live in was in the barrio of Bilaan and that the house would become a permanent school building on the Bilaan Pilot Elementary School grounds. This sounded all well and good until I stepped off the rickety bus in Bilaan about an hour inland from Jolo City. Where my house should have been located were four stakes in the ground – no construction had been started! To say I was dismayed would be a massive understatement. A man approached me as I stood there in shock and introduced himself as Simplicio Ebol, or "Tex" as he was known to all. Tex was in his eighties and was nicknamed Tex because he had fought for the United States Army in the Spanish-American War in the early 1900s. As most of the Filipinos do, he knew English enough to communicate, although his English was more of a "pidgin" variety (most Filipinos speak some form of English as an island-unifying language, although each area has its own native dialect).

Tex told me not to worry as he would see to it that construction started immediately, and, in the meantime, I was welcomed to stay with him and his wife in his house just off the school grounds. I was greatly relieved at his generosity and took my belongings up a wobbling set of stairs. Tex then went to tell his wife of the arrangements. He came back into the room and told me that I was to sleep in his bed, he would sleep on some cushions by the kitchen, and his wife would sleep under the house with the cattle! As with most of the houses in Bilaan, living quarters were on stilts or poles elevating the house, and whatever livestock individuals owned were herded under the house for each evening. Tex had relegated his wife to the hay and straw down below for every evening for the next two months! She, to her credit, thought nothing of it. She cooked every day for me: eggs most mornings (although it is their custom to let them get cold), salads from her garden at noon, and a wide variety of meats for dinner (mostly chicken, but other times monkey, bat, and who knows what else). All evening meals, no matter what the meat was, always tasted of a lot of curry (I guess to hide the gaminess).

Tex was my closest friend in the barrio for all my time there, and he couldn't do enough for me. I miss him more than anyone else there.

Tex and Mrs. Ebol

Don with Tex

Tex with Birthday Shirt

The A.I.D. That Was Lacking Aid

The United States has a number of overseas assistance plans designed to help developing nations overcome poverty and create a higher standard of living for their populace. One of these programs is sponsored by the Agency for International Development, or AID, and evidence of the agency's involvement – or lack of it – was clearly evident on the Philippine Island of Jolo where I was stationed for two years. Let me cite two examples of our government's attempts at intervention which sadly backfired.

Once a month a large tanker transport unloaded pallets of powdered milk onto the docks of Jolo City, and bags of it were piled high on the wharfs in town. The residents of Jolo City and its environs were invited to come to the docks and partake of any of the powdered milk they wanted. There was only one problem: Filipinos do not drink milk, other than fresh goat's milk, and, therefore, did not know what to do with the powdery substance. No one in the agency's Research and Development offices – if, in fact, they had any – had bothered to determine whether the natives knew anything about milk; they would have had to have been instructed, not only in how to use the powder but of its nutritional value for drinking when mixed with water. I saw some Filipinos actually rubbing the powder on their arms and legs as a use for it! However, I have never seen such huge rats in my life by the docks, some as big as large rabbits. Those rats sure knew of the value of that powder!

In a similar misuse of government assistance, in the barrio of Bilaan where I taught elementary education, physical education, and community development, AID had given a substantial amount of science equipment to my school and to each of the schools throughout the island of Jolo. When I started working with students and teachers during my first year, I noticed that the science equipment had been stored on shelves, some still in their original packing containers. When I mentioned this to the teachers, they apologized to me for not using the equipment they were given and told me that if any of the test tubes, burners, vials, and the like were broken while used, the replacement costs had to come out of their salary. I spoke to the principal who said that the rule had been in place for years. I could not believe what I was hearing and told the principal and her staff that we would get a science program going and that if they broke any of the equipment, then I would pay for it myself. If only there had been some teacher training over the years as equipment was being delivered, much of this oversight could have been avoided.

Again, this is government intervention without proper intervention, and the teachers and students were wary of being accountable for damage. Think of how much further along they would all be with familiarity and training!

Don Teaching Science to Grade 3 with A.I.D. Material

Rats Again!

I finally saw my house completed, and I began to furnish it with furniture. My house was made entirely of mahogany, the most common and least expensive of wood in the area, and my tables and chairs were of the same material which I supplemented with a rattan settee set. My roofing was of nipa fronds woven expertly by my contractor, Mr. Castro, who was also the sixth-grade teacher at Bilaan Pilot School where I worked.

After a few weeks of settling in, I was awoken one night by frantic scurring in the kitchen, and when I entered that area, I saw breakfast cereal, flour, and breadcrumbs scattered all over the counter and the floor. I knew it must have been done by rats which had entered through my nipa roof and laid havoc to my supplies.

The next day, I went to the barrio market and purchased two large rat traps which I would set that night. In the evening, I set the traps with some cheese which I had on hand, went to bed, and waited. That night, I heard the commotion again and actually felt the rats run across my feet while I was in bed. Because I learned to sleep under mosquito netting tucked around me, I felt I was protected from their claws and bites.

In the morning, I went into the kitchen area and saw the same destruction of my dried food, but the two traps were untouched. The same scenario unfolded the next night with both traps remaining unsprung.

I decided to consult my Filipino next-door neighbor and good friend, Simplicio Ebol, or "Tex" as he was known to all, and I told him what had happened and what I had done with the traps. He asked me what I used for bait, and I told him I had some cheese on the traps, but the rats weren't lured. When Tex heard that I had used cheese for bait, he roared with laughter and called me a "stupid Americano" (in a joking fashion). 'Here in my country,' he said, 'you can't catch rats with cheese.' He went down to his basement area and brought up pieces of dried fish which smelled horribly and told me to bait the traps with them, and my problems would be over.

That night, I did as he told me, got rid of the cheese, and baited the traps with dried fish and waited. No sooner had I gone to bed when I heard "wham! wham!" as both traps sprung almost at the same time. I was so nervous that I waited until morning to see the traps.

I got up and went into the kitchen with trepidation to see the results of my baiting. There were two very large and very dead rats in the traps, so I silently thanked Tex for his advice and then had to figure out a way to extract the rats, dispose of them, and clean the traps for re-baiting.
I set the traps for a few days more, but there were no further occurrences of food destruction. I told Tex of my success, and he told me to forget my American ways and learn from the natives. For the rest of my time there, I listened to and heeded the advice of my townsfolk.

My Kitchen

Good Old American Ingenuity!

Back in the early '60s when I was a Peace Corps Volunteer on the southern Philippine island of Jolo, there were many volunteers stationed throughout the Philippine Islands, and many of our original training group were sent to the big island of Mindanao for their assignments. Only a few volunteers were female. When each of us was assigned, we were given a "settling in" allowance of $850 to purchase our basic household needs: furniture, bedding, kitchenware, etc.

Many of the women in the Peace Corps, I was told later, either could not continue training in the Philippines or asked to return to the states. They seemed to have had to give up a lot more in the ways of living conditions and arrangements, along with sanitary needs, and only the "really tough ones" were able to stick it out. I knew two of these girls from my training group, and they used good old American know-how to create a lasting story!

These two girls were assigned to live in northern Mindanao, and they did things a little differently, however, and the spending of their allowance became legendary! With their "settling in" cash, they spent a great majority of it on cases of San Miguel beer! What they did was they bought the beer by the wooden case lot and then used the wooden crates to craft their own furniture.

When they had visitors, the conversation always started with the guests asking, "Where did you get your amazing furniture?" and, with the telling, the legend spread throughout the islands. Volunteers would go out of their way to visit the girls and, probably, share a pint.

My House (no beer money!)

Flag Raising from My Back Porch

The "Monkey Man" and the *Quan*

About two months after I had situated myself as a Peace Corps Volunteer in Bilaan, Talipao, Jolo, Sulu, The Philippines, my house was finally completed and furnished to my liking, and many people from the barrio stopped by to visit me and wish me well. On one particular occasion, a man stopped by with a pet monkey on his shoulder and presented it to me as a gift. Of course, I had to accept the gesture, and so a spider monkey became a part of my family. He was about four feet in height with a spindly body and arms which reached down to his knees and had a long, gripping tail. He was secured by a leather collar which encircled his waist and that was attached to a long rawhide leash. I wanted to give it a name, but nothing came to mind. When I showed the monkey to my neighbor, Simplicio Ebol ("Tex"), he roared with his usual laughter and said I should call it "H. A." What did H.A. mean to Tex? He said it was short for "horse's ass" which was the way Tex felt it acted around other people. So, H.A. and I became, literally, inseparable friends as it took every opportunity to cling to me, climb on my head, drag on my leg, and pick at the hairs on my arms. I would leave him outside tethered to my back deck of bamboo, and most of the time he was quiet and serene. At night, however, he screeched a lot as large fruit bats with bodies as big as rabbits, swooped down and dive bombed him on many occasions. As long as I fed him many bananas, he kept quiet. I was hopeful that I could train him to climb one of the seven coconut trees surrounding my property and shake down the fruit, as I had seen other monkey owners do, but H.A. wasn't that trainable.

On days when I had to go into the marketplace, I took H.A. with me with him riding on my shoulder. During one particular time, I needed to speak with someone in the market about a problem I was having with my Coleman kerosene lamp. I did not have any electricity or running water at my house for the two years of my service as a volunteer, and the Coleman lamp was an essential possession for me each evening as I prepared lessons and typed correspondence to the states. I finally found a man who, I was told, could help me with replacing the wick and tuning up the mechanism. When I spoke with him, I learned that he spoke some English along with the native dialect of Tausug, and at that time, I learned the meaning of word *quan* which I soon learned could be roughly translated in English as our "whatchamacallit." Here's the way our conversation, if you could call it that, sounded:

ME: Sir, I need help with my kerosene lamp which won't light.

MAN (after inspecting it): Well, you see, you take the *quan* and pass it through the *quan* before removing the *quan* and then the *quan* will hold your light.

ME (baffled, but trying to be polite): Well, thank you, sir, but could you please demonstrate the instructions you gave me so it will work?

MAN: It is not hard. You need to work the *quan* so that the *quan* can release the *quan*, and then the *quan* will be ready for the fuel.

ME (a bit flustered): Could you please do the work for me? Here's an extra ten pesos for your trouble.

MAN: Of course. Just remember, you have to buy a new *quan* which I do not have in the store, but I'll go get it for you. Putting in the *quan*, however, will not be easy, but I'll do it.

ME (with a sigh of relief): Thank you, sir.

I did not follow any of what the man said, but at least he knew what I wanted. H.A. on my shoulder was laughing away on my behalf. So *quan* became my new "go-to" word whenever my own Tausug dialect lapsed.

Don and H. A

A Play on Language

Within my first year as a Peace Corps Volunteer on the southern Philippine island of Jolo, I began to get a grasp of the local dialect spoken by the natives: Tausug. The Tausug dialect is an Islamic/Moslem/Muslim tongue drawn from an Arabic language and is spoken by all those in the southern islands, as 95 percent of the inhabitants are Muslim, even though most of the rest of the Philippines is a Catholic nation, with English being the unifying language within all of the 7,000 islands in the nation. However, the English oftentimes get warped and distorted and may, in fact, sound like another foreign language!

One of my mentors in Bilaan was Mr. Isahac, an Education Supervisor for the barrio and his assistant, Mr. Boni, who was always at his side. Mr. Isahac was proud of his English mastery, and, like a true Spanish speaker from the islands, he rolled his R's every time he spoke and even corrected my English. He loved the fact that he could beat me in Scrabble more times than not in our daily games. Mr. Boni, however, suffered from a "language malaise" that most Filipinos demonstrated as he constantly confused the sound of the letter F with the sound of the letter P. Mr. Isahac would roar with laughter when he asked Mr. Boni to pronounce the word "flagpole", and he would say "plagfole." Every time Mr. Boni would flip the two consonants, Mr. Isahac would giggle. To make matters worse, Mr. Isahac would occasionally ask Mr. Boni to pronounce the legal phrase "The party of the first part and the party of the second part." You can only guess at what came out of Mr. Boni's mouth: 'The Farty of the Pirst Fart and the Farty of the Second Fart,' which got us all convulsed with laughter. Even Mr. Boni joined in the fun even though he did not know what we were laughing at.

Mr. Isahac explained that almost all Filipinos dealt with this confusion and don't realize it. He said to me once, "Why do you not think Filipinos are not called Philipinos?" That brought more laughter, of course.

Another anomaly of the Filipino's use of language, which can be seen in other languages and dialects of any country, is that they intersperse many English terms within their own speaking and writing. I actually learned most of the dialect of Tausug from the students who were always congregating around my house. A common phrase the kids asked me was *Dile ako sin,* meaning "Give me money." My answer was always *Wai sin*, meaning "No money." So, I learned *Dile ako* as a common questioning phrase. But in their constantly questioning of me, I realized how English terms snuck into their dialect. For example:

Dile ako gilete, meaning "Give me a razor blade." *Gilete* being taken from the American brand name Gillette, their word for any razor blade.

Dile ako colgate, meaning "Give me toothpaste." *Colgate* being taken from the American brand name Colgate, their word for any toothpaste.

Dile ako kleenex, meaning "Give me tissue." *Kleenex* being taken from the American brand name Kleenex, their word for any tissue paper. In English, we have actually done the same with certain brand names, so I understand the connection.

The nuances of language formation and development continue to fascinate me as I enjoy looking at the derivations of vocabulary as a way to further understand a country's communication patterns.

Don with District Supervisors Isahac (right) and Boni

No Shoes/No Service!

The island of Jolo where I served for two years as a Peace Corps Volunteer is located in the southern Philippines in the Sulu Sea. Contrary to the majority of the Philippines, which is predominately a Catholic nation, Jolo and its neighboring islands are mostly ethnic Islamic, or Muslim. The southern islands are actually closer to Indonesia, the largest Muslim nation in the world, and more allegiance was given to Indonesia, than to the Philippines. We volunteers did not know any of this from our training, and so many of the unique traits and customs of this part of the world had to be experienced firsthand, and I made my share of "faux-pas." We did know, however, that Americans were looked up to by the Filipinos because Americans saved them from the Spanish in the Spanish-American War, and, in fact, their national hero is General MacArthur, not one of their own leaders, as he helped write the country's Constitution.

In my first year as a teacher/developer in my barrio of Bilaan, I got to know and work with a number of fine Muslim young men and women, and many helped me immensely in learning the island language of Tausug, which is Arabic in derivation. One of the gentlemen I became friendly with was Hadji Ibram, a holy man in my village. Ibram was called a "Hadji" because he was one of the few villagers who had made the sacred pilgrimage, called a "Hadj", to Mecca, in Saudi Arabia. The journey was a very expensive and risky trip of over three weeks by boat, and many casualties were suffered. Ibram was in charge of the only mosque in our area of Talipao, and I saw him often in the barrio often but never in the mosque.

I decided one day to visit Ibram at the mosque, a place I had never visited before, and so I traveled to the mosque to see him in his element. I opened the front double doors and walked into a beautiful setting with ornate cushions and rugs on the floor and beautiful tapestries hung on the walls and altar of the mosque. I no sooner entered the main room when Ibram appeared quickly from behind the alter brandishing a large machete and cursing at me in Tausug, the native dialect. He noticed it was me, and a big grin appeared on his face as he lowered the sword. He walked up to me, grasped my shoulder, and said, in his broken English, "You are very fortunate that you are an American first and a non-believer second or I would have your head on the end of my sword!" He said that I needed to remove my shoes upon entering any holy place or it would be seen as an affront to Allah. If I were not known as an American, I would have lost my life to him. Thank goodness Hadji Ibram recognized me in the nick of time!

Our Local Mosque

Shoe Polish – Or Is It?

Oftentimes, when my work week was completed at the Bilaan Pilot School, I would walk next door to Tex's and wait for a bus to take me into Jolo City where I spent time at Dr. Cabel's house and occasionally meet two other Peace Corps Volunteers who were stationed on Jolo, Jim, and Nick, who would usually be in town. Lately, because of violence and shootings in their locale of Indanan, they spent more and more time in the city, also at Dr. Cabel's.

In one particular instance, I went into town on a weekend to get, among other things, a tin of black shoe polish which I had in my belongings that I kept at Cabel's as my dark shoes were becoming moldy and quite dirty. Later that Sunday evening, I took a very crowded bus back to Bilaan. Busses left for a destination only when they were completely full, and I mean FULL! Men, women, and children were perched on the roof of the bus, and as many as could were clinging onto railings on the sides of the open-aired vehicle. Then began one of the most hectic and rather amusing bus rides I have ever had.

I was fortunate enough to get a seat in the rear of the bus and squished in a middle seat. On my lap were a few bags, and, in one clear plastic bag, was a tin of shoe polish. As usual, people were staring at me, but it all started when one man next to me began pointing at my wristwatch and saying *Lima,* which in the Tausug dialect is the number five. I looked, saw that it was five o'clock, and said *O, o* to him, meaning yes. He smiled and nodded which must have been a cue for the rest of the people on the bus. An old lady to the left of me began jabbering at me, and all I could do was nod and smile. It seemed that no one on this bus spoke English. The old lady began pointing at my tin of shoe polish and speaking both to me and to others nearby in Tausug. I couldn't understand her, but I knew she was inquisitive as to what I was carrying. I took out the tin of polish and said, in English, "polish" and gestured as if I were rubbing my shoe. I then said *zapatos*, hoping that she might understand a little Spanish, and she nodded in agreement but still pointed at the polish. So, I opened the tin and showed her what was inside of it. By now, everyone in the bus was craning their necks to see what it was. The old woman took the polish, smelled it, and was going to taste it when I motioned to her not to. She understood and then touched it and daubed it on the seat in front of her, but not seeing anything (as the seat covering was also black), she daubed a bit onto my white shirt. I forced a smile while others roared with laughter. She then passed the tin around for all to see (and taste, and smell, etc.). Finally, I got the tin returned to me with only a small amount of polish left in it. A young boy turned around in front of me and spoke, in fairly good English, 'The old woman is crazy,' a fact which I could have told him. She started pointing again, and the young boy said that she wanted to trade her black wallet for my shoe polish tin. I said, *'Di'* (No), and she shrugged her shoulders and got off the bus at the next stop.

When I got back to my barrio of Bilaan, everyone who met me at the bus stop asked me what had happened to my shirt. I had to retell the tale over and over again and hear more raucous laughter as more and more people arrived when they heard the commotion. My bigger concern, however, was with how I was going to get the stain off of my shirt. My neighbor, Tex, as usual, had the answer. He took my shirt, urinated on the stain, and then washed in some "special" water he had. The shirt came out beautifully cleaned, but it took me quite a while to get up the nerve to wear it again!

Bus Route to Jolo City

A Boy with Knowledge beyond His Years

One of the items that the Peace Corps officials distributed to all volunteers was a short-wave radio, and at certain times, we could actually pick up broadcasts from the states which alleviated a lot of our homesick pangs. Unfortunately, on that November day in 1963, we were shocked to hear of the assassination of our beloved founder, President John F. Kennedy, a true champion for our cause to aid others through our service around the world.

Early the next morning, there was a knock on the door, and I opened it to see one of my sixth graders from the school where I taught standing by himself on my front landing. The conversation we had was amazing to me because it was about Kennedy's death. Here is the conversation as I remember it:

BOY: Sir, I am so sorry to hear about the death of your President Kennedy.

ME (amazed that he knew that information): Yes. It is a sad day for our country and for the world.

BOY: Your president was shot in the town of Dallas, is that right?

ME (more amazed): Yes. That is right. It is good that you know of that.

BOY: And Dallas is in your state of Texas, is that right?

ME (continuing to be amazed): Yes. You are right again.

BOY: And Texas is the home state of your Vice President, Lyndon Johnson, is that right?

ME (totally baffled): Why yes. You have gotten the facts right.

BOY (shrugging his shoulders): Well, it's just like Philippine politics!

ME (after some hesitation): Oh, I see what you mean.

What an amazing string of logic by that young man to piece all that information together and conclude with only what he knew from his native country's politics.

At the time, it got me wondering, however…

My Living Room and Dining Area

My Bedroom

An Island Trip with "Bottling" Torres

Even though I was extremely busy with my teaching and community duties in my barrio of Bilaan on the island of Jolo in the southern Philippine islands, I found time (and transportation by overcrowded bus) to go into Jolo City on most weekends. While in Jolo City, I made the acquaintance of Dr. Enos Cabel, a general practitioner, who offered to give me room and board whenever I was in town which I gladly accepted. It was the one time a week that I could get a shower and actually enjoy ice cream. One of Dr. Cabel's friends was a Dr. Isahac, a dentist and the brother of my local educational supervisor who observed me once a month in my classroom. Dr. Isahac was a close friend of a local boxer, Emmanuel Torres, who went by the boxing name of "Battling Torres", and we would watch his fights when available. After every match, win or lose, Torres would hustle to a local bar to partake of many bottles of the local San Miguel beer, and, of course, we accompanied him on many of his post-fight "jags." He became known to us as "Bottling Torres", a nickname which he loved.

One night, after many rounds of beer, Dr. Isahac mentioned that he had been asked to visit the island of Pangutaran, off the coast of Jolo City about 35 miles out in the Sulu Sea, where he would do some dentistry, and he asked us to accompany him. Torres jumped at the chance, but I had to work out some details with my barrio which I did. I did not know, however, that there was no boat service to the island, and learned that we would be covering the journey in a *kumpit*, an outrigger fishing canoe with three other passengers and crew members aboard. Not being the best on any kind of water transportation, I consented, after getting some seasickness pills from Dr. Cabel.

We left on a cloudy but sultry morning with only the most basic of clothing and provisions as the trip, we were told by the captain, would take the entire day. As the *kumpit* rode well in the water, the weather turned sour, and we were soon hit with a downpour. Although it lasted only about a half hour, we were all soaked to the skin, and "Bottling Torres" had thrown up most of the beer lodged in his system making us all the more queasy. As the weather cleared, one of the crewmembers said he was going to get us some lunch and dove off the prow into the Sulu Sea. After what seemed like an eternity, he reappeared with a bagful of tiny sea snails which he proceeded to bang on the bulkhead until the snails' shells shattered. He offered the "meat" of the snails to us all, and the uncooked morsels tasted actually quite good. Torres ate a handful and immediately "lost his lunch."

We arrived at the island and, since we were to spend three days there, we were shown to our quarters. We were to stay in a bamboo cottage built upon pilings out over the harbor inlet without any running water and only a hole in the floor, a "splash toilet", which was our lavatory. That night, at a luau-type dinner on one of the most gorgeous beaches I have ever seen, we drank a local brew called *tuba* which was similar to tequila, including the worm used for "aging." I drank moderately, but Bottling Torres had more than his share, and I had to half-carry him back to the cottage. In a few days, we had to say good-bye to many new friends and prepare for our voyage home. Torres was still hung over, so we laid him in the bottom of the *kumpit* where he proceeded to get sick again. A delightful trip that was one I would take again – but without Bottling Torres!

Our Island Trip

Don with Coconut Harvester

Coconut Harvesting

A Baptism Surprise with a Fiery Ending

One morning in Bilaan, early in my tour of duty, I had an early breakfast and began to get ready to go down the street in my barrio as my housemate, Jack, and I had been invited to a Moslem baptismal celebration. We shined our shoes and wore our *Barong Tagalogs* for the first time. The *Barong Tagalog* is the national formal wear shirt for men of the Philippines and is a loose-fitting silk top, usually white or off-white, with no embellishments or very subtle ones, and was designed to be worn open at the neck and untucked over regular trousers. Our shirts went over very well for the occasion.

Upon arriving at the house, we were ushered upstairs to a large room where there were many beautiful tapestries hung on the walls, and the room was jammed with people. As we entered, we heard religious chanting coming from a circle of men and women at the far side of the room. There were about ten men and four women in this circle at the center of which sat three *Hadjis*, or Islamic holy men, two with white turbans and a third with a white hat. Of the former two, one was an elderly man and the other a high priest, or *Imam*, who would later on administer the baptism.

The tradition here is to first partake of coffee and a large assortment of rice cookies and fried bananas and corn cakes. We were escorted by my Bilaan Pilot School principal, Mrs.

Tulawie, who was her usual vibrant self. After that, we sat around and chatted with many of the guests, all in colorful but formal Muslim dress. All the men (except us) wore brightly colored turbans or hats, and all the women were bareheaded. Many people were crowded outside and tried to view the ceremony.

Finally, at noon, the chanting ceased, and two babies were brought in from the back two rooms where they had been attended to by many women. The babies were wrapped in colorful silk cloth. The high priest arose, and Jack and I crowded in to see. He said a few prayers over the first child as the godfather held him, and then a tray of three glasses was brought to him. These three glasses contained salt, vinegar, and water. First, the priest put some salt on his finger and inserted it into the baby's mouth. Next, the priest took a pair of large scissors from the tray and cut off three locks of the child's hair, one on each side of the head, and one on the front and dropped the hair into glasses of water. The child remained quiet all this time, as were the onlookers. Finally, saying a few more prayers, the priest took a few daubs of vinegar and rubbed it into the baby's hair. The godfather then took the baby into a back room as the chanting started again.

Then, as Jack and I were still watching, Mrs. Tulawie approached Jack and informed him that he was to be the godfather to the second child. A little startled by the suddenness of it all, Jack quickly took the crying baby in his arms and walked into the circle toward the high priest. The other members within the circle were holding paper flowers and ornaments. With Jack holding the baby, the same procedure as before took place. During all of this time, most of the guests were eating platters of food while seated on the floor.

After the ceremony which took over five hours to complete, Jack was heartedly congratulated, and we went into a side room and sat at a large table full of rice, meat, and vegetables. First, we washed our hands in a basin at the table and were told that all the food was heavily spiced in order to "drive any evil spirits" out of us, and we were told to eat with our hands in the traditional native style. The food was fairly delicious and, of course, hot, then we washed our hands again and went back into the main room. Still, chanting was continuing as it had been, we were told, since 7:00 AM.

As soon as Jack and I returned home, we drank about a gallon of water each to "put out the fire." The baptism of a Moslem child is quite a feast, and the food and preparations had been started two weeks ago for this event. According to tradition and Islamic law, a baptism can be held only when the moon is right, and the Moslems here use the Chinese thirty-day calendar. Jack will certainly not forget this day, and he ended up spending as much time with his godson as he could manage.

With Jack at the Baptism

The Ears and the Sore Ankles

During my service as a Peace Corps Volunteer in the southern island of Jolo in the Philippines, I had the good fortune to share my assignment locale with a fellow University of Notre Dame classmate, Jack Green. Jack and I were good friends in college and were lucky enough to be paired together throughout our Peace Corps training and lived together in the barrio of Bilaan where I taught elementary school. Jack was assigned to another barrio further inland, Siet Lake, and had to commute by motorbike an additional 29 miles inland. Peace Corps Headquarters sent him the bike to use, but the roads and weather at times were so difficult that he oftentimes was unable to leave Bilaan, so he often assisted me with my daily work.

Finally, Jack decided to move to Siet Lake to work with teachers and students there, and I inherited his motorbike which we both used when he came back to Bilaan. While in Siet Lake, Jack secured housing in the medical clinic, or infirmary, and became endeared to many of the families there. An interesting aspect of Jack's visage was that his ears were particularly large and stood out from his head a bit farther than normal. The acquaintances he knew in Siet Lake were mystified at Jack's ears and wished that their own ears could be like his. In fact, in many cases, Jack spoke of seeing some childbirths where the family of the newborn child secured tape to the youngster's ears to make them stand out more throughout the younger years of growth in honor of Jack. I attended a few christenings (or, as they were called in Arabic/Tausug: *aqiqah*, or welcoming ceremony) in which special attention was paid to the child's ears. Probably, Jack's claim to fame is talked about to this day!

At one of the ceremonies we witnessed, we were introduced to a traditional Philippine folk dance called *Tinikling*, a ritualistic dance of skill that originated during the Spanish colonial era. The dance involves two people beating, tapping, and sliding bamboo poles on the ground and against each of the other poles in coordination with one or more dancers acrobatically stepping over and in between the poles in a rhythmic high-stepping manner. The bamboo poles produce a clapping sound as they are struck against the ground or against each other with two other poles crisscrossed on top of each other in a musical pattern of three beats. The poles are tapped twice on the ground or on top of each other with the first two beats, then brought together on the third beat. One, two, or more dancers then weave and hop through the rapidly moving bamboo poles with bare feet and ankles. The dancers have to carefully follow the rhythms so as not to get their ankles caught between the poles as they snap closed.

Of course, as honored guests, Jack and I were invited to perform the dance, and, of course, we couldn't say no. After many frustrated attempts, we finally got the rhythm through to our dancing feet but not before many bruised ankles and falls which solicited howls of laughter from the other guests.

We said afterwards that, even if we practiced the *Tinikling* dance over and over, we didn't possess the beautiful rhythms that the native dancers displayed that day.

The Tinikling Dance

A Very Vivid Funeral

Viewing certain ceremonies of another culture takes some getting used to, and when I attended a funeral for a young child, I was unaware of the impact of what I experienced would have on me.

My principal, Mrs. Tulawie, informed me one morning before classes began at Bilaan Pilot School that one of our teachers, Mrs. Seduco, shared terrible news with her. It seems that her nine-year-old son had drowned the previous night in a pond next to Sulu Hospital. Her staff and I were shocked as we knew the boy from the barrio to be as fun loving and carefree as a boy that age might be. All staff members and I gave a two-peso donation to the family, school was shut down for the day, and plans were made to go into Jolo City in the afternoon at 3:30 for the funeral.

A contingent of us left by Jeep (courtesy of the Philippine Constabulary Camp in Bilaan) and, with a few stops along the way, made it into town around 4:30.

We were driven to a house on the outskirts of town, met Mrs. Seduco's family, and viewed the closed coffin. Mrs. Seduco was sobbing heavily, and her face was covered with a black lace. She was wearing an aqua dress with a black fleur-de-leis pattern. We then assembled around a P. C. truck that was to be the coffin bearer, and we walked solemnly behind it uptown to the Catholic church. I learned from other mourners as we were walking that another boy, a ten-year-old "cigarette boy" (seller of cigarettes), had been found in a sack at the airport, and that his head had been cut off. Many mourners were talking of the two deaths as if they were an evil omen and that we should all take extra precautions.

After a brief Catholic ceremony (not a funeral Mass), we congregated again at the rear of the truck and continued to the cemetery on the other side of Jolo City. The cemetery had many unique mosque-like burial markers and other tomb-like structures as both Muslims and Christians were buried there. The coffin was carried to a small cement tomb on top of the ground, and the attendants then took the lid off so that Mrs. Seduce and the others could see the body for the last time. A few of the close family friends had to support her and actually pull her away from the tomb as she strained to get close to her son. The boy was a cute youngster, he had on a white suit, and his mouth and neck were covered with white cotton. His head was clearly visible, and he looked bluish to me. Mrs. Seduco was crying and fingering the body and tried to restrain the men from putting the lid on to the coffin for the last time. Finally, she collapsed and was pulled away, and, as the coffin was slid into the tomb, all the mourners picked up handfuls of dirt and threw them into the tomb, as did I. A mournful wailing erupted from the crowd and lasted for a least a half-hour before suddenly it came to a stop, and people turned to leave.

We rode back to the house where Mrs. Seduco's family had re-gathered, and I sat silently with Mrs. Seduco for about an hour as a group of men began chanting and wailing in another room. During this time, a woman came in dressed in native ceremonial clothing and started telling everyone in Tausug (the native dialect) a step-by-step reenactment of the boy's drowning, complete with body gestures and more wailing. I felt like punching her in the mouth!

Finally, Mrs. Seduco was led off to another part of the house, and the guests were invited to sit on the floor and partake of reception food and drink. Out of courtesy to the family, I stayed at the house for the duration of the evening which did not end until after midnight.

I have attended other funerals, including ones for children, but never had I become so immersed in the atmosphere and customs of a gathering such as this one. Mrs. Seduco did not return to teaching for another two weeks, so I took over all her teaching duties over that time and was praised daily for doing this.

At Mrs. Seduco's Grieving

At the Cemetery

Fly FAST, Die Fast

As a Peace Corps Volunteer, I had to carry out my duties totally on my own, as there were no other Americans in my locality with whom I could confide with any troubles I might encounter. The most pressing need that I felt I had was to maintain my health by what I ate, how I rested, and how I kept occupied in my spare time. I stayed surprisingly healthy, and, like many other local volunteers, every six months I was summoned to Zamboanga City on the big southern island of Mindanao for a physical examination. I looked forward to these trips, as I knew I'd meet other fellow volunteers being evaluated and catch up on what they had been experiencing. The Peace Corps leaders who looked after me had given me permission to fly from the town of Jolo City to Zamboanga for my check-up. Jolo City had a meager airport with only a dirt strip on which planes could land and take off. The only runway was surrounded by six-foot high fences of barbed wire to keep out cattle and other wildlife from interfering with take-offs and landings. At the time, there were only two airlines in the Philippines: a major carrier, Philippine Air Lines (PAL), and a privately owned group of five DC-3s known as Fleming Air Service Transport (FAST). Since Jolo City was not a well-traveled location for the larger air carrier, I had no choice but to fly FAST for my doctor's visit. However, the natives informed me before my first trip that they have a saying: "Fly FAST, die fast" as the carrier did not have the best flying record. Since I had little choice, so, being an impetuous youth, I bought a ticket.

The trip to the big island was uneventful, even though the twenty other passengers and I had some queasy moments with altitude changes. My physical went well although I was given some medication for malaria, but everyone received those dosages, I learned. It was good to see some old friends from training, both from Manila and from Mindanao, and I prepared to fly back to Jolo City. Here's where the "fun" started.

We took off with about fifteen passengers even though there was questionable weather outside of the flimsy craft, but we left without incident. On our approach to Jolo City, I noticed some rain and fog outside of my passenger window, and the plane seemed to be haphazardly rising and falling as we neared the landing strip. Because of the poor visibility, the pilot must have come in quite low as, all of a sudden, the plane jerked to a near halt while not yet on the ground, and I could see strips of wire flapping outside of my window. We slammed down almost on our tail wings and shuttered to a stop. As I disembarked (by gangplank, not by rubber slide), I noticed that our plane was almost totally enshrouded in wire.

We learned later that the pilot had lost some of his bearing and came in lower than he should have. The tail wheel of the plane had hooked some of the barbed wire that surrounded the airport, and the popping sound I heard on our approach was all the barbed wire and posts being jerked out of the ground and covering the plane with wire and wood! I felt like what Navy pilots experience when they land on an aircraft carrier and hook their tails onto the surface cables to stop immediately. Needless to say, I almost knelt down to kiss the ground before I left the airport. For my next doctor's appointments, I opted to take an inter-island steamship, a longer trip but safer.

Near Jolo Airport

Medical Check-Ups

During my two-year stint as a Peace Corps Volunteer in the southern Philippine island of Jolo, I remained fairly healthy, for the most part. Most of my little "irritations" were minor, and I was able to withstand them with medicines and salves from my first aid kit supplied by our government and, in many cases, also using native remedies shown to me by the locals of my barrio of Bilaan. A number of townspeople came to my home when they learned I wasn't feeling well and did everything they could to ease any pain and suffering I had. They would give me lotions to swathe portions of my body along with leaves and bark from exotic plant growth for me to inhale and hold the aroma in my lungs. Muslims of religious stature in the area would sit with me and chant healing incantations while others would place little holy relics in significant areas in and around my house.

However, the United States government told me to go twice a year to a certain location for a physical examination, and a few times, I was asked to go to Zamboanga City on the big island of Mindanao for a thorough check-up. On one such occasion, I stayed at the Peace Corps headquarters near where my original host family, the Cristobal's, lived. During the course of my exam, it was uncovered that I had a mild case of Schistosomiasis, a disease caused by infection with freshwater parasitic worms in tropical locales. The water I was using for drinking and washing had become contaminated from infected animal or human urine or feces. From what I learned, the parasites penetrate human skin to enter the bloodstream and migrate to the liver, intestines, and other organs. It is almost as common as malaria in this area of the world, and, if untreated, could cause delirium and even death. I was told that my illness was at an early stage but that I should go to a hospital for further treatment.

They asked me to fly to Cebu City on the island of Cebu in the Visayan Islands between the big islands of Mindanao and Luzon, so I did as they requested. The hospital in Cebu City was a modern well-equipped facility complete with recreation areas and a swimming pool. I stayed there for three days and was required to take a large pill three times a day to "flush" out my system. From the outset of medication, I felt better, especially from my anal irritation, although everything that came out of me during that time was a bright, lime-colored, "Crème de Menthe" green!

While I was at the hospital, the specialists examined me more thoroughly than they did in Zamboanga City and even gave me a dental examination. When a dental team first looked into my mouth, they couldn't believe what they were seeing. When I was a teenager, I had gone to a dentist near my neighborhood for many years. One day, he informed my parents that he had to retire from dental practice because he had failing eyesight! Upon going to a new dentist who took thorough x-rays, he told me that there was decay underneath each of the fillings in my mouth. I had to have three consecutive days of root canal work, and, in those days, they used liquid gold to fill in the canals. The Filipino dentists had never seen such work, and the entire staff crowded around to see my gold inlays. The head dentist asked me if I had a private dentist come to my home in the states to do such intricate work, and I had to laugh as I said that I didn't.

Luckily, my Schistosomiasis did not return, and my teeth showed no effect from the lack of sanitary conditions I lived with. When I got back to Bilaan, I made it a point to boil water before usage, both for cooking and for washing.

Don Teaching English

“Four Points! Good Grief!”

As a Peace Corps Volunteer in the southern Philippines, I had three major responsibilities: teacher/student education, physical education, and community development. Along with my teaching duties, I introduced the fourth, fifth, and sixth-grade boys to the game of basketball, a sport which was just catching on in Asia at the time. Of course, we did not have a basketball court, basketballs, and hoops/nets, so I had to set things up any way I could. I was able to go into Jolo City and find two hoops, worn but usable, and one of the class mothers knitted two basketball nets out of old fishing netting, but we needed a court to play on. With the help of some parents and teachers, we cleared out a level portion of the field next to our one schoolhouse, and Mr. Castro, a sixth-grade teacher who coordinated the building of my residence in Bilaan, built wooden stanchions and backboards from my rough drawings and attached the hoops. Now, all I needed was a team!

I had played a lot of basketball while in high school and in college, and I found that I had a number of boys who were fairly good athletes. After weeks and months of teaching ball handling and teamwork techniques, we actually had a fairly good squad. On one of my weekend trips into Jolo City, I mentioned my new team in Bilaan to our friends, the local priests of Notre Dame of Jolo High School, and they encouraged me to bring the boys into town to play against some of the elementary-aged players there. The priests, members of the Oblate fathers, even contracted a bus for the team and me to ride into town one weekend. Our team arrived in town (many of them had never been in Jolo City), and they saw, for the first time, an indoor court with concrete flooring. This was an eye-opening experience for them, and they were so awe-struck that they did not play anywhere up to their potential. As more weekend games were lined up, the boys from Bilaan calmed down and got used to their surroundings and played better, although they did not win a single game in the first month of contests.

On weekends in Jolo City, I and some of the priests took part in local adult basketball games, and I played extremely well. In some fashion, word of my playing got back to Peace Corps Headquarters who were planning to assemble a basketball team of Peace Corps Volunteers to play in a Christmas tournament in Manila a few months later. I was asked to join the team and spend a week practicing and playing with other volunteers from the islands. I practiced well and made the starting five as we left for Manila. We were to play a series of three games against three local colleges, and the games were to be held in the Araneta Coliseum, an indoor arena which could hold over 10,000 spectators. Before our first game, I felt really strong and ready, so much so that I wanted to show the fans that I could dunk a basketball, an act which they had rarely seen before. I actually put a type of pine tar on my fingers so I could grip the ball better before dunking, and I made a number of dunks, hearing the "oohs" and "aahs" from the crowd.

This was my major downfall! When the game started, I had open shots but missed almost all of them as I could not get a “feel” for the ball with the tar on my hands. I was taken out of the game. We won, however, and the next night I received a telegram at my hotel from Father Bilman, one of the Oblate fathers who was a big fan of mine. All the telegram said was “Four points! Good grief!” I played sparingly for the final two games while trying to live down my humiliation while learning a harsh lesson on a big stage.

Don with Bilaan’s First Basketball Team

Bilaan’s Basketball Team

Spectacular Baguio City and Environs

During my first Christmas break from teaching at Bilaan Pilot School in Jolo, Sulu in the southern Philippine Islands, I spent ten days in the capital city of Manila and in the Upper Luzon areas of Baguio City and Bontoc. I was fortunate enough to have qualified for the All-Peace Corps basketball team which played a series of games in Manila with games ending on Christmas Day. A number of Peace Corps Volunteers were in Manila at that time, and it was good to see many of my old friends from our stateside training days.

After the games, a few of us decided to travel up to Baguio City which we had heard was similar to a New England town high in the mountains of the big northern island of Luzon. A couple of friends and I arrived at Tutuban Railroad Station in Manila at 6:00 AM and settled in for a smooth five-hour ride in a modern air-conditioned coach to Baguio. We passed Angeles, Tulac, San Fabian, and finally at 11:30 pulled into our last stop: Damortis. From here, it was straight up from the seaside locale of Damortis into the mountains, so we contracted a car and driver at the station, the car being a 1952 Plymouth. We wondered how the old car was going to make it through the hairpin turns and sharp upgrades, but we chugged along. We followed a deep gorge through the mountain passes and saw beautiful purplish-green mountains cut by a raging stream at the bottom of the gorge. Thankfully, the road was in good shape except where an occasional landslide had made the going a little rough.

After forty-five minutes by car, we reached Baguio, a quaint little town over a mile above sea level. We stopped at a hotel recommended to us, but all rooms were taken, so we went to the Vallejo Hotel in the center of town. The rooms were small and dingy without private bathrooms, but at five pesos a day, we didn't complain. As I was registering at the front desk, two Filipino boys walked in, and we struck up a conversation with them. They offered to show us around Baguio. Their names were Boy and Pingot, and they were cousins. After I unpacked, we met them in the lobby and got into their black Mercedes 220. We stopped into a few souvenir shops and saw the exclusive Baguio Country Club where Boy was a member. We had dinner there in a pine lodge with logs smoking in the fireplace and with animal heads mounted on the walls – quite a different Philippine atmosphere than I had come from. The club was perched on the side of a high peak, and we did not see any coconut or banana trees at that altitude. There were trees similar to aspens, and they were turning color like it was autumn back in the States. The climate was clear and wonderful with the temperature hovering between fifty to sixty degrees, and I wore a sweater at dinner.

During a dinner of tenderloin steak which Boy signed for, I learned that Pingot was employed by Sampiguita Studios and is a movie actor who got a starring role in his first picture. His stage name is Vic Vargas, and he had a box-office smash in his first role in a Tagalog film, *Diegong*

Tabak. We talked about the film industry and the draw of Philippine cinema in the Tagalog language which is the main native tongue other than English. He is overly modest and not swellheaded in the least. He told me that if acting interferes with his studies as an accountant, he would drop acting. His next movie was to be filmed on the big southern island of Mindanao near Zamboanga City, and since I am stationed in Jolo, I might be able to get to see some of the scenes during shooting. The film is entitled *Bird of Paradise*, and he will star as a native islander with Tarzan-like qualities.

After dinner, we left Boy and Pingot and walked through town where we saw some Igorot native tribesmen clad only in loose-fitting light robes and begging on the street.

The next day, Boy and Pingot invited us to accompany them on a trip to Bontoc to see the rice terraces which are cut symmetrically into the sides of mountains. Filipinos call them their "Eighth Wonder of the World." It was a long winding trip through more mountain passes, and on the way, we passed Our Lady of Lourdes grotto at the highest attainable peak outside of Baguio, and we could see the waters of Leyte Gulf off in the distance and saw the myriad reds and blues of the *vintas* (fishing boats) below. We also saw the Philippine "Summer White House" where President Diosdado Macapagal stays away from Manila. I was told that he was here now for Christmas vacation. His palatial-like mansion is beautiful with manicured, sloping gardens and a long water causeway leading up to it.

Bontoc is spectacular, and we viewed the terraces from many different vistas. Many rice planters and harvesters were at work and singing. Their voices rose up the mountainsides and were pleasant to hear. Boy and Pingot had other plans for tonight, but Pingot told me he would be in Manila during the next week, and we made plans to get together.

When we got back to the hotel in Baguio, a few other Peace Corps Volunteers had arrived and told us about an American eatery called the Halfway House located in Camp John Hay, a U.S. Air Force base nearby. The best thing about the Halfway House is that, by using our Peace Corps I.D. card, we could gain entrance. We went there with them for dinner and drinks and learned it operated just like an Officer's Club in America, so all food and drinks were wonderful bargains! The club was set up with an American décor and had a Latin-American combo playing. The menu was all-American fare, and prices were in dollars and cents. My drink was a Manhattan (only thirty-five cents!), and dinner was a chopped sirloin steak. Our entire bill for eight of us was only around thirteen dollars, but we could pay in pesos which was about fifty-four pesos, forty centavos.

The next day, we had breakfast at the Pines Hotel, and some of us went back into Baguio to Burnham Park where a few of us took a small sailboat out on a lake for about an hour and then drove little motor cars around an oval.

Some of us went back to dinner at the Halfway House at Camp John Hay again, and I had delicious spareribs and a few Martinis. I took Boy and his friend, Nannie to dinner there and watched a very creative floor show with a man impersonating Buddy Holly, Bobby Darin, and Harry Belafonte in excellent fashion. The highlight of the evening was a man juggling and then balancing a *kris* (ceremonial sword) on his front teeth. I went back to my room early as I had to get a car ride to the train station to return to Manila.

The trip was a nice break for me from my teaching duties, and I had many tales to tell upon my arrival back in Bilaan as most of the people in the barrio had never even heard of Baguio City.

Kumpit on Beach Near Baguio City

Road to Bontoc

Volcano Near Bontoc

In a Pig's Eye to Denvir

On one of those lazy weekends in March when all my teaching and clean-up work was complete, I again grabbed a bus to take into Jolo City for a stay with Dr. Cabel and his family, but the bus was going to spend an hour at the Bilaan Market, so I was fortunate enough to hear that a truck from the P.C camp in the area was leaving for town, and they would take me in. As usual, the truck was loaded to overflowing with people, Coke bottles, bamboo, grain sacks, and hemp, or *copra* as they call it. As I moved cautiously to the rear of the truck, I stepped on what I thought was a large grain sack, but as I stepped on it, the "grain sack" moved and groaned. The sack was, in actuality, the biggest sow I had ever seen lying on its side and strapped to a bamboo pole.

We rode with reckless abandon as if the truck was empty and got into town in thirty-five minutes. Unfortunately, the sow suffered a bloody snout when she pounded her head on a shattered glass Coke bottle and sprayed me with her blood.

At Cabel's, I had mail waiting for me and also saw in the Sulu Star newspaper that the U.S. Navy ship, *USS Charles Berry*, on a goodwill tour out of Subic Bay in northern Luzon, was to dock in Jolo later that day. That afternoon, after watching the docking maneuvers at the wharf, I learned that many of the sailors were going into town in order to play softball against the Jolo All-Stars. As the game started, another PCV from another area of the island was asked to umpire, and I was asked to substitute at shortstop for a few innings. One of the Oblate fathers from the Notre Dame of Jolo High School told me that one of my Notre Dame University classmates was an officer on the ship and would play in a local basketball game later this evening. I knew all of the local basketball players who would play that evening, and their captain, hearing of another "real" Notre Dame graduate in town, invited me to play with his team against my classmate, Quin Denvir.

After arriving at the gym early, I met Quin, and we spent some time talking over all that had transpired since our graduation in the spring of 1962. He informed me that he was the Supply Officer for the *Charles Berry* and that the ship had left San Diego three months prior and had been to Hong Kong and was going to go back there, then to Japan, and then back to the states in May. He told me that the ship is a small destroyer with ASW (Anti-Submarine Warfare) armaments.

At the conclusion of the game, he invited me to come on board the next morning during visiting hours, as they were to leave port around noon that day. After the game, Quin went back to the ship to shower as there was to be a dance and dinner for all officers at the newly opened Moongate Club and also an enlisted men's dance at the high school gym. Quin and I met up again at the Moongate and were entertained by speeches from the Governor of Jolo Island and the Mayor of Jolo City as well as Lieutenant Commander Weeks and Ship's Consul Lane who were ship-riding with them for a while.

Quin and I spent a good portion of the evening swapping stories and tales. He had to be back on board the ship by midnight, so I accompanied him to the wharf. The ship was all lighted up like you might see on a naval postcard, and I watched him snap a salute to the deck watch as he boarded.

The next morning, I went down to the ship, and since Quin was the Supply Officer, I knew that I could get cigarettes cheaply. I boarded the *Charles Berry* in a slight drizzle and Quin met me and proceeded to give me a tour. He showed me the fantail (the aft main deck) and the 0–1 deck (different from most destroyers which have only three decks). As we passed Quin's office, he showed me the supply room, and I spent some of my dollars getting Pall Malls, Marlboros, cigars, candy, etc., to share with my fellow PCVs and the Cabel family. Quin then took me to the bridge, and I saw the pilothouse as well as the anti-submarine missiles given to the Navy by Norway on an experimental basis.

We then went to his quarters where I showed him pictures of Bilaan, and then we both went to the officer's wardroom and had coffee and talked. Before I realized it, the "clear all decks" horn sounded, so I quickly said good-bye, as did Mr. Lane who was leaving the ship and flying to Zamboanga City this afternoon. I was the last one off the ship as the gangplank was already being drawn up. The ship finally left Jolo City at 11:00 AM after backing in and out for half an hour before finally getting under way.

It sure was great to see Quin and catch up on some old times. It's a small world to see a Notre Dame classmate in Jolo City, of all places. The Navy treated the townsfolk and me quite well, and the Jolo locals put on a fine showing for the Navy personnel, as well.

Jolo City in the Distance

Road to Jolo City

Bar Fight – Or Not

Occasionally, when my housemate, Jack, and I were in Jolo City for a weekend, we were offered many opportunities to drink and dine with the many friends that we had made in town. Our favorite gathering place was La Jota where their sizzling steaks were beyond compare! Another place that had newly opened was the Sky Room, a more jazzy setting with modern décor and a more youthful clientele. If we went to dinner at La Jota, we would inevitably end up at the Sky Room later on in the evening for drinks with friends and listen to good music.

On this particular evening, Jack had some places to go, so he couldn't meet me for dinner at La Jota but promised that he'd meet me later at the Sky Room. I arrived at the Sky Room where I waited in the lobby for a half an hour before he entered. We were then shown to a table up front near the stage, but before we could sit, our Chinese friend, Hock Go, spotted us and offered to have us sit at his table. As courteous at this might sound, this was probably our worst mistake of the evening, but we could not refuse an invitation from our good friend. We sat down with Hock just to the right of two female singers preparing to go onstage and perform. We had a few beers and paid little to no attention to three loudmouth guys sitting behind us. They fit right in as most of the customers that night were loud and drunk. We were chatting with Hock and his three friends when one of the guys behind us came over to our table and started a heated conversation with Hock in Tausug, the native dialect of our area. Although I couldn't understand most of what was said, I could see that Hock was getting pretty heated up. All of a sudden, beer bottles were pushed off of the table, and then the throwing started. One guy threw a bottle at Hock, missed, and the bottle splattered against the pillar right next to us. Then Hock threw a bottle which also missed its mark. I had been talking to a Philippine Constabulary sheriff at our table just then, and he called for order as he drew his pistol. I later learned that these three loudmouths had drunk up about 24 pesos of beer, but they only had 12 pesos among them and were asking Hock for a loan. Hock had refused, and then the action started. I had just observed two policemen come in the door with pistols drawn when Hock threw the only punch of the fight, a beautiful right to the jaw of the drunkest of the three, and he was so drunk that it took him some time before he reacted to the pain.

Jack and I had left our seats immediately and were now standing in the opposite corner away from the stage while the nervous combo of musicians struck up some music. Just at that moment, there was a blackout all over Jolo City, if you can believe it, as there had been heavy lightening all evening, and a bolt must have struck the Jolo Power building. I stayed by a window, as I was sure shooting would break out. Flashlights flickered on, and I looked for Jack but couldn't find him. I heard him call out for me from the back of the room, so I made my way over to him. Then one of the policemen told us to stick close to him as he had a gun. That was the last thing we wanted to do, so we moved further toward the back near a kitchen entrance. At that moment, the lights came back on, and we saw that Hock and his oppressors were in the act of being escorted off the premises.

Jack and I quickly settled our account and left right behind the policemen. I had never seen so many guns drawn in any situation such as what we had experienced.

The next day, we heard many stories about the growing reputation of the Sky Room as a “hot spot” for other reasons than it should be. Hock told us later that the Sky Room was developing a sordid reputation and that he would no longer go there. He said that incidents like this would force the club out of a legitimate business and force them to go into “catering with hostesses”, as he put it. All of us crossed the Sky Room off our list for future reference.

Jolo City and the Sky Room Bar

My Ad Hoc Conference Presentation

In the spring of my first year as a Peace Corps Volunteer on the island of Jolo in the Philippines, I had begun to settle into my role as teacher educator, community developer, and quasi "role model" of America abroad. I was experiencing for the first time that people were listening to what I had to say and wondering why I said what I said throughout a given day. I was asked to speak at numerous functions on a wide range of topics, many of which I knew little about, but because I was an American, I always had a rapt audience.

On one particular week, I was invited to attend the Second Annual Regional Echo Family Conference in Jolo City for the advancement of family and educational development. I acted, with about eight other people, in the role of consultant to about 200 teachers from all over the island. I had been invited by my Bilaan Pilot School principal, Mrs. Tulawie. I was to be in charge of one of the three conference groups; our group was to focus on the development of the moral and spiritual responsibilities of the family. We were given prepared questions, and the conference was keynoted by the governor of the island and local mayors. These speakers went on and on just to show that they felt they were great orators.

I was sitting and listening to one of the speakers who was rambling on about economic problems in the home when suddenly one of the bigwigs at the conference came up to my seat and asked me if I would please speak to the delegation and give them an American viewpoint. On what, he didn't say. Fortunately, all attendees spoke the islander's version of English, so I could be understood. I don't mind speaking in front of large audiences, but I would like to have had time for some preparation. Before I could gather my thoughts, I was brought on stage. It was my first time ever to give a speech without any notes in front of me as well as not having any definite knowledge of the subject. I could not speak from experience about managing a family's economy as I was not married and was also not an economist. All I could give were my views on the subject.

Suddenly, I realized that I had spoken for 45 minutes, and the audience was still alert and listening, maybe because I threw in a few amusing anecdotes. When I finished, three of the bigwigs rushed up to me and congratulated me for one of the best speeches of the conference, and they asked my permission to use the text of my speech in the newsletter and report of the conference. They look bewildered when I told them I had no text. But one of them brightened up and ran off and then came back telling me that the conference recorder had taken down my speech almost word for word. I couldn't wait to read it and find out what I said!

The next day, the conference continued, and I wore my new *Barong Tagalog,* the formal ceremonial dress shirt for all male Filipinos, and I was ushered into a side-room and given a manila (of course) envelope with schedules and groupings for the day's activities. As the consultant for Group One, which was to be concerned with improving family responsibilities from a moral, spiritual, civic, and economic standpoint, I was to coordinate all responses and summarize them at the conclusion of our group's work. I was fortunate to have my group's personnel all from Bilaan, my barrio. We were to answer seven questions ranging from religious training in the home to such questions as: *Is a Filipino man incapable of committing himself to one woman for life?* We had gotten to only our third question when our day's activities were called to a halt, and we convened in the large auditorium to hear reports and closing speeches. I was instructed to sit on the stage with other guest speakers, and my speech of the day before was cited often.

After receiving our "Certificates of Attendance", the conference adjourned. Many of the bigwigs invited me to a dinner out and they told me that they would love to have me as a guest speaker whenever the need arose.

On reflecting back to the conference proceedings, I concluded that many Filipinos are great showmen and imitators of whom they considered to be great orators. What could have been accomplished in a single day took two, and work was not completed even then. Filipinos have no peer when it comes to sidetracking or beating around the bush on a question, and it was all I could do in our sessions to keep my group focused on our task. I guess I failed in that regard, but I learned later that the other groups had gotten through only their second question!

Don with Mr. Castro and Grade 6

Bilaan Pilot School Graduation: The Highs and The Lows

As I concluded my first year of teaching and teacher instruction at the Bilaan Pilot School, I was asked to assist in the planning and implementation of the school's graduation ceremony which was to be a combination of oratory, dance, awards, and music. I had spent some time with my guitar composing an alma mater song to be sung at the graduation. The principal and all the teachers agreed to practice it with the sixth grade and also to sing it themselves with them in preparation for the big day. The school song is entitled *Hail Bilaan,* and the words are as follows:

HAIL BILAAN

Soft Sulu breezes whisper 'round thee
The regal palms bow to thy fame.
Bilaan, the birthplace of our knowledge,
Help us to cherish more thy name.
And when our schooling days are over,
We see our fondest hopes and dreams.
Together, let's shout "Hail Bilaan,"
Star of Sulu and the Philippines.

I used as the melody an old camp song I was taught when I was about ten years old, and the rhythm was easily followed.

My housemate, Jack, and I dressed in our *Barong* Tagalogs (formal wear) and went to the school grounds where a stage had been set up outside of the Grade Six classroom. The ceremony was to have started at 9:00 AM but didn't get under way until 10:00 as my supervisor, Mr. Isahac, didn't arrive until then. We sat on the stage with other dignitaries. Mr. Rizal Tulawie, the ex-mayor, was the guest speaker and spoke for almost a half hour in Tausug (the native dialect).

The graduation ceremony started off well, and the graduates (about 20 of them) wore khaki trousers and white shirts with a red rose pinned to the collar. Two students, winners of a school-wide oratorical contest, gave declamations which were well received by more than 100 spectators present. The traditional folk dancing began with students (mainly girls) moving and gliding to the sounds of stringed instruments and *gabong,* a group of brass percussion instruments varying in size and tone. Then there was a comedy show and a skit (pageant), plus song solos and choruses performed by select students. Mrs. Tulawie, Bilaan's principal, then presented the students for graduation, and I was to stand on the stage with her and shake the hand of each graduate. Then, as a surprise to me, I was asked to say a few words on behalf of the students. Luckily, I am not shy about speaking before crowds and gave some ideas to students about taking the next steps in their lives. I tried to intersperse some *Tausug* into my talk in English which elicited some laughter all round.

Then, there was a series of glitches! Mrs. Tulawie was just about to dismiss the students and spectators when she remembered my graduation song, which was to have come much earlier in the program, and half the crowd was on their way out of the area when the song started. They sang the song in a half-hearted way and a bit off key. They were probably a bit over-rehearsed and felt a little tired of the song after over a month of practicing each day. Then, our tape recorder which my housemate, Jack, was handling wouldn't work, so there was no record of it for the future. On top of all that, my name had been overlooked in the printing of the program as being a part of the teaching force.

After the ceremony, Jack and I were invited to the Grade Six classroom for a small lunch of rice and chicken, and then someone started up some music, and Jack and I "twisted" with some of the female staff members. It seemed like at every place we were invited to, we were asked to dance, and The Twist was the dance of the moment. Jack and I did as was expected of us, but neither of us was great at it, yet we received shouts of encouragement and applause as we swayed to and fro.

Awarding of Diplomas

Graduation Stage

Graduation Dancers

Life With Bindo Alpa

During my teaching experience in Bilaan Pilot School on Jolo Island in the southern Philippines, I worked with teachers and students in a Grades 1–6 schoolhouse with four classrooms. With six different grades, the Principal, Mrs. Tulawie (one of the six wives of Mayor Lincoln Tulawie), decided to have Grades 1 and 2 taught in an "out-building" on Mayor Tulawie's property. As I taught and interacted with the student body in Bilaan, I soon realized that the majority of my students were female, almost 90% of them in fact, and the age range of the students was anywhere from seven years of age to 21 years old. I soon found out that the male population of school age children was mostly out working in the fields and on the coconut plantations around the barrio, as was their custom.

One of the few male students who quickly came under my eye was a young man named Bindo Alpa, a Muslim, who had persuaded his family to let him attend school and take part in all school activities. Bindo was an extremely bright and able student who always came to class prepared and continually asked for more work, especially in math and science. He was a sixth grader, and, upon graduation, was presented with the honor of being Class Valedictorian, the first male to have been presented with that prestigious title in the history of that school. Yet, Bindo had no plans after graduation, so, with his parent's permission, he allowed me to present him to the Oblate fathers running the Notre Dame of Jolo High School in Jolo City as a rising student in their lower school. He had never been to Jolo City, so I toured him around and had him meet many townspeople who could assist him along the way. Bindo started at NDJHS that fall and immediately impressed his teachers with his work ethic and endeared himself to his teachers and the Oblate fathers. I paid Bindo's tuition of $19 each semester, bought his books and his uniform, and became his unofficial guardian as I set up housing for him, as well.

When it came time for me to return to the United States, Bindo and I had a tearful good-bye, and he promised to write to me every week. While he was attending high school in later years, I heard often from the Oblate fathers that Bindo continued to shine in the classroom, earning various honors, and even was named the Commandant of Cadets for the military youth there. He continued on to college on a scholarship from the Ateneo de Manila University in Manila, a long way from his childhood home. I continued to support him financially and emotionally from my home in New Jersey, and he sent me many letters and photographs attesting to his continued success in college.

Alas, I lost track of him soon after college, but from his last communications to me, I learned that he would be entering the military. If this isn't a "rags to riches" story, I don't know what is!

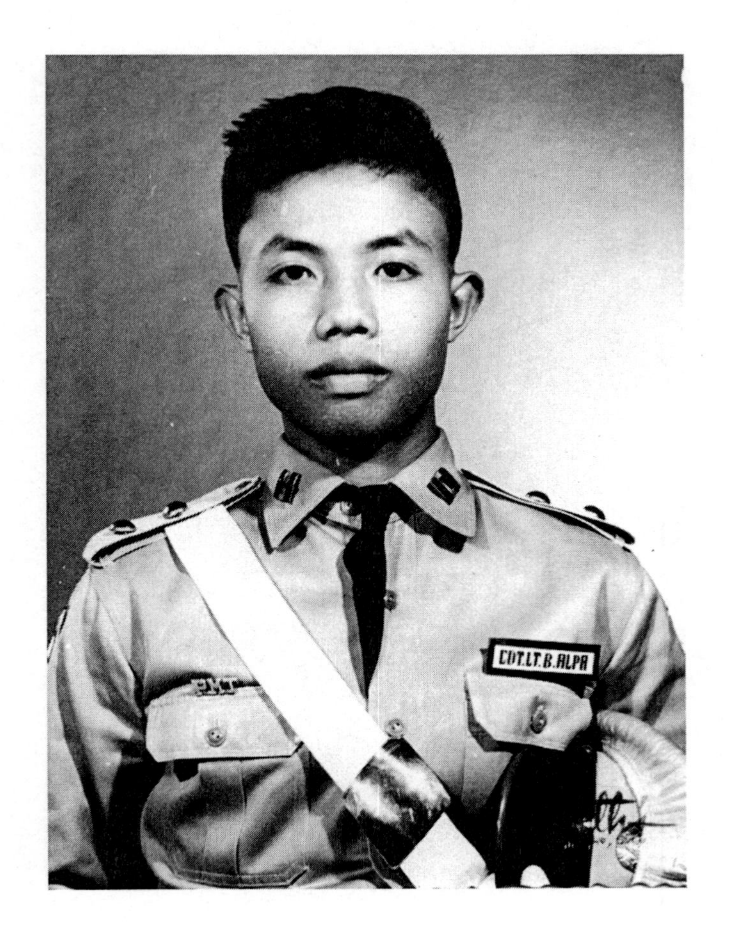

Bindo Alpa at Notre Dame of Jolo H.S

Bindo Leading His Command

Bindo Receiving a Commendation

Problems and Fatalities

In preparation for my tour of duty with the Peace Corps, I had to undergo much physical and mental testing by the Corp's screening committee. Not only did I have a complete body physical, but also went through a series of respiratory and circulatory examinations. Besides that, I was asked to take a number of mental tasks to check on my "sanity" along with aspects of judgement and decision making to make sure that I was fit for the job. I expected all of that and came out quite well.

One area I did not expect that created much curiosity on my part was when two F.B.I. agents came into my little town in New Jersey and began inquiring with my friends and neighbors about "just what sort of a guy I was." They went to the local police station and the town hall to view any past records which might create a problem for my resume. They even went into a few local bars to see what people knew about me. Luckily, I came out clean and risk-free, according to their report. I found out during conversations in my training with other volunteers across the country that everyone had experiences of this nature in their hometowns, and most just laughed the experience off as a type of "preparation overkill."

However, as we continued our service, I learned of some problems that other Peace Corps Volunteers were experiencing which, I guess, were not expected. One of our volunteers had to be sent to Manila for a tumor operation, two other males in our group were diagnosed as alcoholics, and one girl who I knew quite well wanted to be sent back to America, so she began to steal things and became a kleptomaniac. Two other girls got into much trouble when they began dating natives in their barrios, and they were sent back to the states when it was learned that parents and relatives of the men whom they were seeing threatened the girls with their lives. It just goes to show that no matter how thorough the screening of an individual can be, human nature can never fully be analyzed.

From others in the northern islands, I learned of a volunteer with a sadistic desire to become the first Peace Corps Volunteer to die in service, and he starved himself and put himself in harm's way in many instances, and eventually in our first year he died. We later learned that another volunteer in Thailand had died in service a few weeks earlier, so our Philippine volunteer couldn't even claim that "fame."

To make matters worse, while we were spending a weekend in Jolo City at the home of Dr. Cabel, word came through to us through the local paper that there had been a bad airline crash in Davao City, and a good male friend of mine from training along with another girl from our group had perished. There were no survivors. I was visibly shaken by the paper's unscrupulous detailed account of the state of the bodies. These newspapermen seem to stop at nothing to sell a story! The male volunteer roomed right across the hall from me in training and was famous for his riotous imitations, especially of Eleanor Roosevelt.

A few months later, we were saddened to learn of the passing of another volunteer in Cotabato who died as a result of an overdose of malaria suppressant. Again, we were forced to come to grips with our own mortality. At the time, we learned that eight volunteers had died throughout the world, and four of these eight had been serving in the Philippines. Out of these four, three of them were members of our service contingent: Philippines Group VII.

Don with Bilaan Teaching Staff

"Thoughts"

There were many times when I spent evenings in my barrio home contemplating my life back home in Glen Ridge, New Jersey and what it was I was missing from there. Often, I would just pick up a pencil and start writing verses to help me cope with my new life, but my thoughts about kids my age, especially girls, helped me create this poem as I dreamed.

THOUGHTS

Whisking wind blowing ghosts into curtains;
Music: soft, swaying, sensuous
People conversing – oblivious,
I am thinking.

Past pleasures giving fleeting specters;
My mind: plodding, prying, patient;
Gone years – noticeably,
I am smiling.

Brown bangles kissing hazel orbs;
My girl: young, yearning, yielding;
Lens focusing – gradually,
I am weakening.

My molding, restricted to my mind,
Hurts: irritating, irrational, ironic.
Damn the past – completely,
I am damning.

I am speaking,
Naturally – fully attentive.
The past: trials, tribulations, triumphs;
Dissected delicately from the now.

Composed by Don Yates as a Peace Corps Volunteer,
Bilaan, Talipaw, Jolo, Sulu, Philippines (1962–1964)

Reflections

Nearing the completion of my service time as a Peace Corps Volunteer on the southern Philippine Island of Jolo in the Sulu Archipelago, I finally took time to think back upon my total experience, both as a teacher in the Bilaan Pilot School and as a representative emissary of the United States. These times have flown past so quickly that it seems only yesterday that our group trained in San Jose, California, Manila, and Zamboanga City and then were spread out on our assignments across the 7,500 or so islands of this Southeastern Asian country. I have been enlightened in so many ways as to my own strengths and weaknesses as I grew into my responsibilities in the field of education and community development throughout the region.

Initially, I have been so pleased that the barrio of Bilaan and the surrounding community have accepted me into their homes and workplaces and recognized, for the most part, that I could make a difference in their lives. Much of what I had tried to do needed to be "sold" to the populace, and every day, I found myself attempting to get my thinking and work ethic out to the men, women, and children and have them respond in a positive manner to my presentation of the Three Goals of the Peace Corps:

- To provide technical assistance when asked
- To promote better understanding of America
- To promote better understanding of other people by Americans

To me, I couldn't have performed my duties without the support and assistance of my neighbor and dear friend, Simplicio (Tex) Ebol. Tex was there for me upon my arrival when my house had not been completed, and he and his wife took me in for over a month to stay with them. I can't think of a day where he didn't try to help me get acclimated and feel comfortable in a strange environment for me. His assistance to me was of daily importance to my overall well-being.

My School Principal, Mrs. Tulawie has been overly cooperative and supportive of my school and community work and shared extremely practical advice so I, at times, wouldn't embarrass myself. She and her husband, Mayor Lincoln Tulawie, included me in many of their social gatherings and family events, so much so that I felt a part of the Tulawie clan.

My housemate, Jack Green, a college classmate and fellow PCV trainee, helped me in so many ways by being a great sounding board for ideas and plans within our two-year mission. He was good at getting me acclimated and acculturated, and with his booming personality, was a great influence on the students and adults we interacted with. His straightforward approach to our seemingly unending problems helped save us from many mini-disasters, and his never-ending good humor made the hours fly by. Jack was assigned to the barrio of Siet Lake and had to commute by motor-bike on an almost daily basis until he finally decided to move to Siet Lake permanently, and I became a bachelor for my final year in Bilaan.

As I sit at the dining room table writing, I can see rain clouds slowly approaching over the coconut grove at the rear of the Grade Six classroom. My back is to the road, and on the right side of the house, near the District Supervisor's Office, I see two yellow birds that look like American goldfinches, but these birds fly upside down occasionally and perch upside down and fly at a standstill like a hummingbird. I am aware of animal and insect life around me constantly. On the whole, the flora and fauna are larger and more colorful than I am used to seeing in the States. Chartreuse green lizards a foot long, spiders with a body the size of a quarter, bats the size of hawks, and mosquitos with bites like bee stings are vivid memories which I will take with me.

And so I say, to all the Filipinos and to the Philippines, *Mabuhay* (Tagalog for "Good Fortune"), and I hope my work in your wonderful country has been acceptable in your eyes and, therefore, has increased the prestige of America abroad!

Fish Nets Drying in Jolo City

Fish Nets Drying in Jolo City

Epilogue – "Journals of Peace" Presentation

Donald C. Yates (Philippines 1962–64)
Monday, November 21
3:48 pm

WORDS CANNOT EXPRESS nor emotions imply the impact that my years as a Peace Corps Volunteer in the Southern Philippine Islands still holds for me now after over 25 years. We were a special breed, we early volunteers, and many of us postponed or forsook budding careers in business and industry to share in this opportunity of a lifetime. Most of us were caught up in the zeal expressed so often by our late President, John Fitzgerald Kennedy, and saw an opportunity to assist those less fortunate than ourselves by "getting our hands dirty" in the many developing nations of the world.

Yet, other motives prevailed upon us, as well. I, for one, looked upon Peace Corps service with, perhaps, a selfish motive. I felt that if I could teach for two years under the most adverse of conditions in a leaky, termite-ridden schoolhouse in the middle of a jungle halfway around the world and return to the States with a strong commitment to continue teaching, then I would know that it had to be in my blood to be an educator.

Let me say that the spark of the sixties has remained with me to this day. There is no question in my mind that my Peace Corps experience enabled me to strive for excellence in my own educational pursuits. I am a holder of three Master's degrees and a Doctorate from Columbia University and have taught and administrated at almost every grade level in both public and private schools and in urban as well as suburban settings in the State of New Jersey.

At that time, however, it was not easy for me to make any type of momentous decision, much less a two-year commitment as a stranger in a strange land. I was only a mediocre student at the University of Notre Dame; however, I looked upon the Peace Corps training experience at San Jose State College in California and at Zamboanga Normal College in the Philippines as perhaps even more important and meaningful than my four years as an undergraduate.

From these two training centers, only the "cream of the crop" were sent into the Sulu Archipelago, south of the large island of Mindanao, and only four of our Group VII members were sent to the island of Jolo where the populace had not seen a white man, other than missionaries, since the liberation from the Japanese in 1946; a tiny hour-glass shaped island where national allegiance was more often seen toward the Moslem/Islamic nation of Indonesia rather than toward the more Christian government in Manila.

An incredible learning experience followed as I diligently led these people by good example and exemplary conduct. Becoming conversant in a little-known Arabic dialect in order to barter in the marketplace; realizing certain Moslem taboos in worship, in eating, in marriage, and in death; living without electricity and running water for two years; having a pet monkey to climb palm trees and throw down coconuts; and just basically surviving are just some of these instances which could fill volumes.

In order to convey more fully the deep meaning of these two years as we gather in Washington, D.C. to commemorate our late president and founder twenty-five years after his assassination, allow me to share in this moment of memory by relating a final excerpt from my Peace Corps journal of the early 1960s:

On Tuesday, I left Bilaan for good, emptying my house completely of all my earthly possessions. I gave my sala set to Miss Asgal as she will get married next month, and it will be their wedding present. I gave my bed to Mrs. Kadil as she and Roger have just had a daughter and need it badly. The rest of my things I sold and made about 90 pesos which will go to the family of my number one student graduate this year whom I will support in the city of Jolo at Notre Dame High School. His name is Bindo Alpa, and he is our first male valedictorian in five years. He is exceptionally bright, and I don't want him to miss out on a good education because of his poverty. He has earned a scholarship at NDHS because he is a first honors student but will need money for school expenses, uniforms, books, and the like. He will start high school in August, and, if need be, I will support him from the States as tuition is only 50 pesos, or about $16.00, a semester.

Leaving Bilaan was the hardest thing I have ever had to do here, as I have so many close friends whom I may never see again. I know I'll never see "Tex" (Mr. Ebol) alive again as he is 74 years young now. He shrugged off my leaving in his usual jocular manner, but his dear wife cried, and it was all I could do to keep from shedding a few tears of my own. I really choked up when the truck pulled away from the house, and half the barrio was there waving goodbye, including my entire sixth grade. It will be equally as hard to leave Jolo City and Dr. Cabel's house which was my home away from the barrio. It is difficult for me to continue this discourse, too draining.

Since that final week in the Philippines, I have returned to the States with the desire to teach and administrate. I was extremely pleased to have been invited to Washington, D.C. in March of 1965 by the then Vice-President Hubert H. Humphrey to participate in a conference with about 200 other returned PCVs to discuss how each of us has best been assimilated back into Western Culture after our experience abroad. The time spent with President Lyndon B. Johnson, Sargent Shriver, Harry Belafonte, and others was a fitting climax toward a fuller understanding of the demographics of crossing cultures.

Now, as I complete my 27th year in the field of education, I cannot help but reflect on my Peace Corps days, especially on this significant occasion. I, and my colleagues alike, often reflect upon the immortal words of another great American, Thomas Jefferson, as he said:

Educate and inform all of the people, for they are the source of our strength and our freedom.

Peace Corps Memorabilia

PEACE CORPS IDs

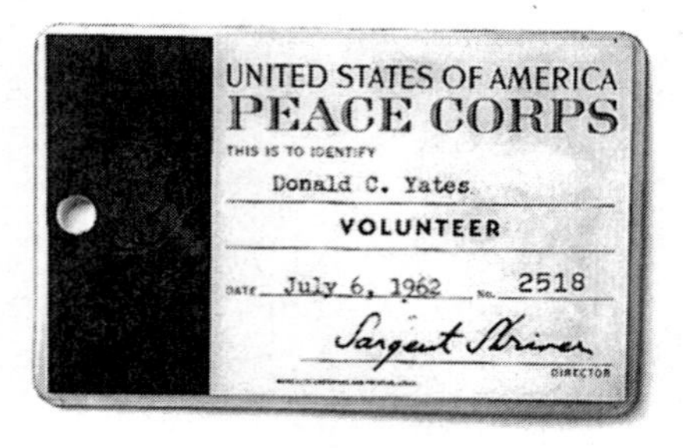

UNITED STATES OF AMERICA
PEACE CORPS
THIS IS TO IDENTIFY
Donald C. Yates
VOLUNTEER
DATE July 6, 1962 No. 2518
Sargent Shriver
DIRECTOR

PEACE CORPS
Washington, D.C. 20525
This is to certify, in accordance with
Executive Order No. 11103 of April 10, 1963, that
Donald C. Yates
served satisfactorily as a Peace Corps Volunteer.
The Volunteer's service ended on 5-15-64
Record no. 014524
Date of issue 6-15-64
Sargent Shriver

Letter from President J. F. Kennedy

THE WHITE HOUSE
Washington

July 18, 1963

Dear Mr. Yates,

You have recently completed your first year of service in the Peace Corps.

At home and abroad, the Peace Corps has been recognized as a genuine and effective expression of the highest ideals and the best traditions of our nation. You and your fellow Volunteers have made that judgment possible.

I am proud of your participation, and I trust that in your second year of service your conduct and performance will continue to reflect credit upon and the Peace Corps.

Sincerely,

John F. Kennedy

Invitation from Sargent Shriver

Mr. and Mrs. R. Sargent Shriver
request the pleasure of the company of
Mr. Donald C. Yates
for cocktails and buffet supper
on Saturday, March sixth
at six o'clock

R.S.V.P.
The Peace Corps

Edson Lane
Rockville, Md

Note from Congressman Peter Rodino

PETER W. RODINO, JR.
10TH DISTRICT, NEW JERSEY

COMMITTEE ON
THE JUDICIARY

Congress of the United States
House of Representatives
Washington, D. C.

DISTRICT OFFICE:
COMMERCE-COURT BUILDING
10 COMMERCE COURT
NEWARK, NEW JERSEY

You're quite the celebrity after that newspaper spread – I'm sure it pleased you very much.

Thought you might like to have my copy for your scrapbook.

Sincerely
Peter W Rodino Jr

P.S. If ever I can be of service, please do not hesitate to get in touch with me. PWR Jr

Letter from Vice President Hubert Humphrey

THE VICE PRESIDENT
Washington

February 6, 1965

Dear Mr. Yates,

I would like to invite you to participate in a Conference of Returned Peace Corps Volunteers to be held in Washington on the weekend of March 5–7. President Johnson has asked me, as Chairman of the Peace Corps National Advisory Council, to convene this Conference, to consider "opportunities for further service…in all parts of our public life."

The Conference will assemble a representative group of former Peace Corps Volunteers and leaders of American Education, business, labor, government, and other major areas of our society. It will be a working conference. Small groups of Volunteers and leaders in private sectors and government will discuss experiences, needs, and ideas. The workshops will develop findings and recommendations. Their report will be submitted to the president, to members of the congress, private leaders and others for possible action.

President Johnson has emphasized that returned Peace Corps Volunteers represent a “great new resource” to the nation. You are one of about 3000 returned Volunteers. By the end of this year, 6500 volunteers will have returned; by 1970, there will be over 50,000.

I need your help to make this conference an historic launching point for new and improved service to the nation.

Under separate cover, the Peace Corps is sending you a pre-conference questionnaire, a proposed agenda and other particulars. Your prompt reply to the Peace Corps questionnaire will be appreciated.

Thanks and best wishes.

Sincerely,

Hubert H. Humphrey

Hubert H. Humphrey
Mr. Donald C. Yates
238 Forest Avenue
Glen Ridge, New Jersey

Article from *The Glen Ridge Paper* about Don in the Peace Corps

ON YATES, Glen Ridge's first Peace Corps volunteer plans a day's schedule for his Philippino students as he is shown in the native Philippino relaxing dress, the pjadjong.

He Exemplifies the Corps

– By Barbara Kukla

From Glen Ridge to Bilaan would be considered a strange way in anyone's book to start a new career, but for Donald C. Yates of 238 Forest Avenue, it was most logical. For Don returned this June after spending two years teaching in the Philippines with the Peace Corps.

After graduating from Notre Dame University in 1962, Don decided to make teaching his life's work. 'I had read about the Peace Corps,' he reflected, 'and decided that if I could handle those kids, I would have the devotion and zeal to go on.' And he did.

Don received his initial Peace Corps training at San Jose State College in California where a group of 150 volunteers gathered for a rigid series of courses which would prepare them for their work as teachers' aides in the islands. The courses included instruction in the native Filipino language: Tagalog, Philippine culture, secondary (English) language methods, American history, a study of communism, and tropical health and diseases.

After a 10-day home leave, the volunteers left from San Francisco to the islands with stopovers at Hawaii, Wake Island, Guam, and Manila. Then there were two more weeks of orientation before the group parted and Don arrived in Bilaan on the island of Jolo where he was to teach English, health and science, and physical education.

For Don Yates, there were many new things to which he soon became accustomed...living in a thatched hut, eating such exotic foods as sheep's eye soup, raw snails, and banana flower salad...just being halfway around the world from home.

But the one thing that was outstanding was a personal concern for the people of the Philippines. He describes it as "culture shock", the sheer poverty of people that is unimaginable to Americans and the American way of life.

'You hear about poverty, but you don't believe it until you see it,' he explained.

As an aide to a native teacher, Don spent six to six and a half hours a day in the classroom. He found the Philippine people very intelligent and his students well disciplined. The only drawback in the educational system, he noted, was that all subjects are bound by the political system, even at the elementary school level.

Outside of his regular classroom responsibilities, Don organized teacher classes, speech clinics for teachers and parents, and science methods classes. Although the science teachers received equipment from the Agency for International Development, many of them were afraid to use it, because they had to pay for broken items out of their salaries. Don encouraged the use of the equipment by teaching the correct usage and promising to pay for any breakage because "it would be my fault for not teaching you correctly."

An active participant in sports while in college, the young American was a player and a player coach for several teams in Jolo and was selected to play on the All-Peace Corps squad which was undefeated in 1962 against some of the top American teams. In 1963, he coached the same team. And, as a town project, his sixth-grade boys built a basketball court.

Don taught in an old school with two pre-war buildings, a new industrial arts building, and a large garden where the students conduct projects. The faculty of eight is headed by a woman principal.

Since there are no junior high schools in the Philippines, students are graduated from the sixth grade and then enter high school. Many, however, are so poor that they must drop out of school and go to work. But there is a thirst for education in the Philippines, and many students return when they can. "One of the boys in my sixth-grade class was older than I was," Don said, stressing this point.

Bindo Alpa, too, is a poor boy. He ranked first in his graduating class, and with the assistance of Don Yates will go on to high school in Jolo City.

Don is the first Glen Ridger to enroll in the Peace Corps program and the first to return home. Traveling first through Europe, he reached home in June.

He is the son of Dr. and Mrs. Glen L. Yates. His father is a physician at Mountainside Hospital. He has a brother, Glen Jr., a sophomore at Northwestern University, and a sister, Margo, who is a secretary for the National Newark and Essex Bank.

Although he confessed that he missed the opportunity for intelligent conversation and privacy ("the kids were always peeping in the windows 24 hours a day"), Don sums up his two years in the Peace Corps as "the most rewarding experience of my life." He and a fellow volunteer are presently editing the notes from a diary of his first year in the Corps which will probably be the first such publication by a Peace Corps worker.

From *The Glen Ridge Paper*, September 17, 1964, reprinted in full with permission from Worrall Community Newspapers, Inc.

Peace Corps Diploma

UNITED STATES OF AMERICA
PEACE CORPS

Hereby commends

Donald C. Yates

for dedication to his country and service to the people of

Philippines

as a Peace Corps Volunteer

from June 15, 1962 to May 15, 1964

DIRECTOR

Peace Corps